MW00895994

Go

Copyright @ 2022 Shelley A. Leedahl

All rights reserved. No part of this publication may be reproduced, stored in a
retrieval system or transmitted, in any form or by any means without the prior
written permission of the publisher or by licensed agreement with Access:
The Canadian Copyright Licensing Agency (contact accesscopyright.ca).

Editor: Donna Kane
Cover art: Kimberly Kiel
Book and cover design: Tania Wolk, Third Wolf Studio
Printed and bound in Canada at Friesens, Altona, MB

The publisher gratefully acknowledges the support of
Creative Saskatchewan, the Canada Council for the Arts and SK Arts.

Library and Archives Canada Cataloguing in Publication

Title: Go / Shelley A. Leedahl.
Names: Leedahl, Shelley A. (Shelley Ann), 1963- author.
Description: Poems.
Identifiers: Canadiana (print) 20220184089
Canadiana (ebook) 20220185514
ISBN 9781989274675 (softcover)
ISBN 9781989274699 (PDF)
Classification: LCC PS8573.E3536 G6 2022 | DDC C811/.54—dc23

radiant press
Box 33128 Cathedral PO
Regina, SK S4T 7X2
info@radiantpress.ca
www.radiantpress.ca

SHELLEY A. LEEDAHL

Go

For Peter Mutafov

and in loving memory of Jim Herr—
character, legend, father

Also by Shelley A. Leedahl

The Moon Watched It All

I Wasn't Always Like This

Listen, Honey

Wretched Beast

The House of the Easily Amused

Orchestra of the Lost Steps

Talking Down the Northern Lights

Riding Planet Earth

The Bone Talker

Tell Me Everything

Sky Kickers

A Few Words For January

"The heart is a wild and fugitive creature.
The heart is a dog who comes home."

-Helen Humphreys, *Wild Dogs*

—

"It has been a long hill, heart."

-Jan Zwicky, "Courage," *The Long Walk*

1 . What is Good

So Much I Don't Know about U-hauls
2. Ways to Be Happier
4. Snake Walk
5. I Keep Returning to the Blue-lit Places
6. Goodbyes
8. Saskatchewan House
9. Tina
10. Upon Meeting Owen Wilson in an Organic Grocery Store
11. Pennies
13. My Father Collects Broken Instruments

Stalking Windows as the Story Develops
15. Song for the Homeless as We Drive to Ruth's Chris Steak House in a Red Convertible on a Thursday Night in June
17. Deluge
19. The Pantry of All There Is
21. Alberta Avenue
23. Sometimes
24. Bees
25. More Words for Winter
27. The Beauty of His Feet on Christmas Morning
28. Our Therapists Agree
30. Janos
31. What I Left in that City

The Ocean Will Do That
33. Let Us
35. Sunshine Coast Series
37. The Dead Zone
38. Smuggler Cove Marine Provincial Park
39. The Heart is a Red Umbrella
40. Five Day Visit

I Wait for an Epiphany and Don't Expect a Bright Light
43. Places
44. Rue de Menoncourt: Notes on a Global Home Exchange
45. Missing Exits
47. Porrentruy
49. Can't Write Today
51. Alfama
53. Salema

What I Like About You
57. Reno Air Races
59. Oarlocks
61. Hottest July on Record
62. Tsawwassen
63. Lopsided
65. Perseids
67. After Tony Hoagland's "Reasons to Survive November"
69. Late December

Forget the Old Arguments
71. Forget the Old Arguments
72. After Ross Gay's "To the Fig Tree on 9th and Christian"
73. Ladysmith: Gratitude 1
74. Ladysmith: Gratitude 2
75. Ladysmith: Gratitude 3
76. Ladysmith: Gratitude 4
77. May
78. The Quiet
80. Thanksgiving 2020
82. Christmas Prayer
83. How To Love Your Life

Manitoulin Suite
85. Manitoulin Suite

91. Notes and Acknowledgements

What is Good

Wednesday afternoon hikes with Rachel,
who lives, as I do, in awe
of sprays of grass
that end in star-flowers.

Pine scents. Ravens, and the birds we guess
through the memory-pull of song.

Multi-coloured salmonberries. Plucking season.
Appetizer before the full blush of blackberries.

Arbutus, peeling one page at a time.
They say *Red*. They say *West Coast*.

It is good to sit on a ledge above the town
that is above the ocean. To point at islands
and hear nothing but tree-bones.

Silver lichen is good. And the rainbowed tinder fungus.
Also salamanders, manifesting rain.

So Much I Don't Know about U-hauls

Ways to Be Happier

Take yourself outside, observe
the light rain on the pond.

Don't worry about your hair
or canvas shoes—just hover there,
like these whole notes
of solitude
are what you allow yourself
every afternoon. Or morning,
if that's your preference.

Let the fish entertain
with gilded flashes. After a time
you'll notice the bee balm
with your right eye, then the bees
themselves, burrowing
inside blossoms, their little sleeves rolled up
above their wee bee elbows.

You'll find black-statued angels
where you least expect them.
Also white ones. And the sprites
that are scary laughing men.

                There, in the window—
a cat named Percy watches
you watching her, a tree
superimposed over the feline's reflection
as if her fur's morphing into leaves.

Don't fear the snake who lives in the rocks:
see him sticking his skinny neck out? He doesn't care
about you. (The robins guarding their nest
absolutely do.)

Trees are good friends any time, and textures
are truly old languages. Don't fret

if you don't know all the words yet—
                      some say "hens and chicks,"
and others "chicks and hens."

See how the garden's full of cradles
and woman-shapes? The urn, bowl
of pond, wheelbarrows?

If you don't have your own garden, steal
into one at nightfall.

Oh little one, faceless to me now.
You can't wholly trust the world, but the garden
only knows how to love you.

Snake Walk

—For Logan

Why do we love to discover them
along the prairie train track? Garters
long as your arm—
                    even longer—
baking on gravel or curlicued
in the shin-tangle whipgrass.

Where we are truest. Closest.
Soft-stepping down the rail line—
    mother/son, mother/son, mother/son—
prey to darting avocets
and badger holes. Unsticking ticks
from each other's legs
and bronzed necks. Ears tuned to
thin-whistled grass blade, eyes finessing
tell-tale stripes.

We count fifty-three today. New record.
You photograph my veiny fist
full of intact snakeskins.
Like Hydra, you say.

I'll find a long flat box, mail one
to your sister in Montreal, another
to my old lover, the rest I'll release—

                    sheer ribbons—

to the indifferent village of wind.

I Keep Returning to the Blue-lit Places

Thanksgiving two days gone
but already snow lights the village
                    and the garden's remains:
swiss chard and crimson wildflowers.
It feels more like Christmas
than Christmas. Trees
appear purposely decorated
in sparse, tri-coloured leaves. And this blue
light, a wash I never notice
inside the envelope of cities.

Yesterday I entered the woods
                    and listened for wing-sounds,
expecting a barred owl.
(Only two rabbits, grey-brown
with striking white feet. Not easily hidden.)
I heard children
                    or the ghosts of children
across the spring-fed lake.

                    Who will darken my door today?

I wake with lists: trim back
the ribbon grass, fill the tire with air.
I don't recognize love or sparrows
evenly spaced on the powerline.

The blue light lifts, the weeping sky
abates; maybe today
I will be the better woman.

                    Listen—

The clock. And cedars
scraping their nails against window-glass.

I move city to village to metropolis.
Trade one life in for another.

Everything is everything else.

Goodbyes

1.
Penultimate night in this house
with the sadness I've nurtured
diseasing the walls
with black mould.

Sign on the lawn proclaims the home is for sale.
I am for sale.

Who could want this dirty-kneed one
who knows only hard work
and finger-thorns?

The garden's raspberries. So dark and ripe
they are halfway to wine.

2.
I will not get to see the calla lilies bloom.

3.
Neighbour Eileen knows I'm not eating.
She brings a bowl of lemon potatoes—
slippery with butter,
and the best thing I've eaten.

Light on the crabapples.
Heliopsis: yellow stars behind eyelids.

4.
Wolf approaching.
I fasten the windows and wait.
Now in the spruce trees,
now rattling the giant sunflowers.

Only a storm after all.

5.
A lone bald eagle against the cavernous sky,
as if prairie's confused with coast.
Harbinger? Happenstance?

6.
Mint on my hands,
dirt in my teeth.
Ticks like snaps on my skin
in the night.

7.
Behind the raspberries, the compost heap.
I bash the hell out of a mouse
with a rake and feel
the blind joy of killing.

8.
Swing around the campground for a one-last-time.
Find the blown-out body of a whitetail.

9.
Farewell village café.
Farewell dripping eavestrough.

The end-time has come for moon-gardening.

Saskatchewan House

An offer is on the table.

Rooms where I lived a little
but mostly just learned
to be quiet as snow-stars
on a barley stalk
in the field I stared into
until blinded, until almost nothing
remained. The coffee cup's heat
a small, still pet
within the parentheses
of restless hands, so busy at weeds—real
and predominantly real.

Almost every meal alone
at the antique dining table—
                    its milky surface—
another thing
undealt with.

Perhaps the gold-brown carpet can be saved.
What does one need, really?

Black plates stacked in cupboards,
a few second-hand bath towels.
Books and rakes and instruction manuals,
my appliances the wrong colour
for this century. The Heintzman piano
that knows only carols and Beatles' songs
in the easy-going key of C.

So much I don't know about U-hauls.

Only an offer, and yet I make much of it.

Tomorrow I'll know more
about something
for sure.

Tina

You're dying a bell, droving us back
from disparate poles to Meadow Lake—
                    one pizza parlour, a bowling alley.
That stallion on Main rearing in perpetuity.

Northern girls together
throwing jacks and playing jump rope
in our one-streetlight town,
with a rodeo, a stampede
of snow.

Those who could not return for your wake
connected by phone—
                    the western sky beaded in satellites.

Three of us stood beside your open coffin—
                    grim bridesmaids—
while five hundred mourned
in the gym, a nebulae of faces
I knew I should know
through the woodsmoke,
the drumming, Cree prayers.

Doreen stayed the night with your body—
                    I only made myself touch you.

Upon Meeting Owen Wilson in an Organic Grocery Store

1.
Paia, Maui.

A family of four suited up like astronauts
in neoprene and helmets.
We tore down the Haleakalā volcano
on sturdy bikes in the rain.

We surfed. Snorkelled with turtles
and the depths were lunar.

We drank like professionals.
Passed out New Year's Eve
before "Auld Lang Syne."

2.
Owen was buying a takeout coffee.
We glanced, he smiled
like a friendly puppy.

I followed him down a sandy lane for a bit.

It's a short story.

3.
Last time I went anywhere
with my husband and adult kids.

We were shattering. Sunburned. Flipflopped. Tragic.
We were down to the freakin' dregs.

Pennies

I'm completely out of wine.
Always like this, nights I need to pretend
I own a New York loft and am one of those
tall, lithe women who's perpetually thirty-two
and paints abstracts in happy colours, paints
her lovers' bodies in abstract colours
and is continually blissful, barefoot
and posing before floor-to-ceiling windows
in panties and an unbuttoned white linen shirt.

The best thing about today should not have been
spotting nine pennies in the mud
when I stepped from my car. I brought them in
to one-day polish, one-day tell a grandchild
about these little coppers
that feel good in the palm—

                              or elsewhere—
skin-wise.

       See a penny, pick it up.
       Penny for your thoughts?

Where will all the old expressions go
now the penny's obsolete?

On the flip side, I've sold my house
to someone who deals in diamonds
and my bank account will soon be fatter.
I'm frightened of the sum
in the way one might wince
near lashing animals in zoo cages.

Money is fire: I am convinced
I should not touch it.

I showed no foresight re: the lack of wine.
I stand before the pantry wondering why
I possess three roasters, seven rolls of plastic wrap
and a blood pressure monitor
surely I'll not need for another decade.

Oh, and I recently turned fifty.
It took a lot of wine
and pennies
to get here, all the way from 1963.

Subterfuge. Cities are best at it.
Somewhere not here there's sophisticated jazz
and small white lights, sparkling.

Here? Moonlight on flint in a creekbed.

My Father Collects Broken Instruments

My father collects broken instruments
the way other men pocket pens
or tack baseball caps
above tools in a garage.
Two guitars with strings whiplashed or missing,
a trombone lacking the decency
of its mouth. My father plays nothing
but his own whistled breath
and can no longer stand
for more than a minute, still
he haunts yard sales and flea markets,
returns with a silent mandolin,
a clarinet soon forgotten
and dismembered
behind a granddaughter's bedroom door.

Photos immortalize my brother
faking gospel
with a dented trumpet, reflect toddlers
mad-dancing with decrepit tambourines—
oh, baby, we shook some joists.

The sum of a lifetime, scored with non-banjos
and un-harmonicas. My family
in strange hats and banging gongs,
creates disasters and calls them songs.

Stalking Windows as the Story Develops

Song for the Homeless as We Drive to Ruth's Chris Steak House in a Red Convertible on a Thursday Night in June

                    Night peels off
and I am wide-eyed at 4 a.m., the window
above my desk framing a bricolage of rooftops,
chimneys and ah, now the spruce
are waking too. It sounds pretty
but it's not, nearest neighbour's home
one part corrugated aluminum
he's hammered down himself.
Buddy looks like someone whose knees hurt
well before it rains.

                    Sometimes we talk
in small sentences
though I can't recall his old-country name.
One morning he slid me lilacs
across the fence, once he lent
a strange kind of flute
I had no intention of playing.

                    Now here come the magpies
outdoing traffic but on par
with industrial wind. Nothing smells like carnations
here—not even carnations.

                    Last night, finally,
my partner and I used the gift certificates
for Ruth's Chris Steak House. Imagine spending
almost $200 on a little fish and wine.

Driving to Jasper Ave down 95th Street,
                    more homeless
sprawled outside the House of Refuge Mission
than I could scope, everything mystery

and molasses here. Mariana Trench
of men and women
wearing old blankets

                         and oxymoronic donations
that do not fit.

                         One bony couple
entwined like the last two standing
in a dystopian movie—
                         couldn't see her face
but surveyed a math of ribs
in a bikini top,
and they just held on to each other—I want to say
                 for dear life—
and swayed a little less
than the spruce tops, more
                    than a highway mirage.

Deluge

Symphonic rain, but this is no lullaby.

Ear to the pane. Ear to the past. One tires
of her chapters: windows and weather stories
through the solstice of years.

              One becomes old
recalling rain, the kids barefoot, smiling
and steeping in it
beneath dripping elms
in a different city: a drama set hard
as initials in cement
that refuse to wash away.

Decades, however, dissolve
as mysteriously as mist.
Currently I am lured outside
in the throat-hold of night
to consider blossoming puddles
between spikes of new onion
              and the pink lupines
that follow my impenitent course,
man to man, inner city to inner city.

Only these flowers—
    the seeds transported across borders
    inside the pages of books—
do not fail me.

—

            The sky over Edmonton:
titanic, tissued in clouds.
It defers to the wheedling wind
               and sirens
needle the dark suede of hours
into the shape of a lunging dog.

And you, latest dreamer—
                   naked and blissful
among feather-down pillows
plump as loaves
from the Portuguese bakery—
do not miss me
in my sock-and-gown creeping
across this garden of shadows.

(I startle a sex worker at her trade
behind our garage
when I set out the reeking trash.)

—

Come, morning. Sooner is better.
And let us civilians splash to the library
beneath bold umbrellas, whale-skinned
in slickers and gumboots
                  like children, like actors
in a maritime movie.

We'll sit close to windows in coffee shops
admiring transients with wet smiles
for no one.

The Pantry of All There Is

The hour is shy of 6:00 a.m.
and the sky's spitting kernels of rain,
yet there you are kneeling
in the sodden garden, a penitent
among chickweed and fine boas of asparagus,
mud-clots glommed to your cuffs
where they'll dry and later flake—
oversized blisters—
across carpets and kitchen:
this you will also not notice.

Consider the comical weight
of your cheap black sandals, frescoed in gumbo
halfway to cement.

                    —How did you arrive at this?

A girl who held staring contests
with the acid sun, chased squirrels,
and believed in edges.

You grew up, discovered
you understand less than a slug.

                    —

Lady of the shredded heels,
what do you make of this perennial routine—
the metallic-zipper-slide sirens
closing the gates on the ends of each hour,
stopping the gymnastics of lives,
and why start your weeding in the corners
where nobody ever sees?

                    —

Violet, rain-hooded morning.

Heavy-eyed, you-should-see-the-other-guy sky.

How dystopian
when one's ankle-deep
and sinking. When no one requires
even the smallest things—
                    a cup, a kiss—
from your pantry
of all there is to give.

Lady of filthy fingernails,
your trowel's gone missing again,
swallowed by soil or the goutweed
you slice away
with fundamentalist persistence.

Alberta Avenue

1.
Phosphorescent clouds over 93rd Street:
     underlit dust, purpling. They belong
in a picaresque about thunderheads.

The soundtrack is neighbourly. Eastern Europeans
beneath an umbrella speaking Czech.
(Could also be Polish.)

Blueberries on the table
where buddy sharpens the homemade axe—
               I do not make these things up.

It takes me back
to last night. Playing guitar—
songs from the binder, songs from the twine.

My voice: a pair of broken hips. Slow-
mending, and temperamental
with dips in temperature.

We served corn-on-the-cob, a little burnt
in the foil; counterpoint
to the sirloin shish kebobs.

2.

The Battleford apple is weighted with fruit
scabbed in elegant rot—
          it's that late in August. Hot as teapots.

Punching-bagged, clown-shoed.
I download apps to help me sleep; white noise
is available in colours

Addicted to weather warnings,
I stalk windows as the story develops.
Clouds smithereen, like dandelions.

Sometimes

On rain-full days, my lover
finds me transfixed
at the window, arms crossed on the sill,
chin cupped. He understands
it's about the garden,
but he knows nothing of seedlings
and I don't try to explain
how the neighbouring lupines—bleeding crimsons
into one another—prove
a higher power exists. Volunteer pansies—
they do this, too. A kind of tie-dyed
coalescence, each slightly different
and ever beyond mortal artistry.

To be civilized is to enter one's garden
and take time
to cut and arrange flowers
for the dining room, the unremarkable sill
above the sink, the piano-top.
Perhaps to sit a while on a bench or step—
                    still damp with dew—
and be present
with the heralding crows.

                —Do I make too much of this?

Gardens don't prevent wars
or heal shattered relationships, but sometimes
this modest patch of inner-city gumbo—
        immune to the hovering police helicopter,
        siren's perpetual screams—

fills the heart-shaped vase
through the hours of a nine-day rain.

Bees

Feel twice my age, at least.
Limbs grizzly. Impending winter
and Stepford wifing.

The downstairs tenant
never leaves the house
and I swallow his stones, too.

My still-green tomatoes
on towels across the kitchen
because aphids
coat the garden like frost.

Make myself lace into running shoes,
thunder into the river valley.
Hope someone will dare
to cross me. A man on a bike
is assaulting women
in Edmonton: I can no longer
even be afraid.

Squat beside a shopping cart
beneath Jasper Ave's wooded bank
to release my finicky bowels.
Don't see the ash-haired bear
with his blanket
and den of cardboard
until I am wiping with leaves.

Eyes like oil slicks. Hands frayed
and twitchy. I want him
to say something, or slam
his mouth on mine. I want
to taste the dull tin of blood.

Twenty minutes from home—
            I finger my house keys.
Sky is smoke-blue, mothy.
The traffic on Jasper is bees.

More Words for Winter

An extra hour of sleep, snow-ushered in,
as if time and the elements colluded.

Yesterday we were raking
last leaves, tarping patio furniture.

            One day into you
and we're web-surfing foreclosures
on Vancouver Island.

The window draws my turtled eyes
to the colourless sky and raspberry canes
bent under the fresh white weight.

I am six. Twenty-four. Forty-nine.
Winter, I know you like the scars of me.
Your season calls for snowy owls
and unburdening.

The neighbours did not get their trampoline packed.
Nail-sized icicles decorate eaves
on a dilapidated garage.

Snow. The every-year-heavier shouldering.

A woman sweeps off her compact car
and it stops resembling a polar bear.

Skeletal plum trees throw graphic shadows
against the cedar fence.

The snow-garden softens: cat-prints
across the deck become suggestions,
become larger nothings.

Four o'clock dark, and my breath leaves
a vague O on the glass.
O one day. One day I may move
a thousand miles west, but winter—

        raspy gasp—
        ice-flakes beneath streetlamps—
        the wet-sock slip inside boots—

I know you'll find a way
to stick with me.

The Beauty of His Feet on Christmas Morning

Outside the covers, beneath my lips.

Paper and bows from last night's unwrapping
crushed into balls on the carpet.
Stockings emptied. Board games
await the afternoon.

The coffee's unmade,
and his son sleeps in jeans.
Rabbit tracks pock the snow
between townhouses. Spruce stand there
like shepherds, like the souls
of our beloved dead.

Possibly I have died, too. Another spent candle
among the ceramic nativity scene,
the donkey and cow
each missing a right ear.

—

The world glows.

Daylight on his feet, the gospel
of snow. A rain of crumbs
where we sat late into the night
eating Hungarian biscuits.

The poinsettia's leaves.
The silent guitar.

The delicate sculpture of an arch.

Amid mania and flurries—
holiness and champagne,
these two bared flares. Innocent
winter birds, keeping me there.

Our Therapists Agree

We should kill this thing
with a gutting knife. But I'd never know
the slope of your back
as you set lettuce seeds
between a rift of black soil,
how coastal rains would heal the cracks
in your winter-skinned hands.

There'd be no large, short-haired dog
to train together
and take on leashless hikes—
tree-strobed, scented in pine needles,
blackberries, and salmon
bear-pawed from the stream.

You wouldn't sample the photogenic meals
I'd learn to make, and so long
to your broad-shouldered wake in the lane
as you'd swim like a champion past me.

I'd never get to see you hold a baby.
You couldn't know the pleasure of a campfire
at my family's log cabin—

        stars sprayed like charms,
        smoke-tangles and lake sweaters,
        loon-songs endorsing the gloaming.

I would not get to meet your Budapest.

I could no longer stroke your arms
or read aloud poetry you don't understand
but seem delighted to fall asleep breathing to.

Only four months, our therapists repeat
in offices far across this frigid city.
We *should heal quickly*.

We swallow their words
like white bread, like Scripture.
You cage my hands, and we pray.

Janos

While you were texting old and future lovers
back home in Hungary, I hid
behind sunglasses and beat down the blocks
until sidewalks ran into snowfields,
welcomed wind to blow knife-holes
straight through me.

(Two Mormon missionaries in black pants
gave me their business card,
asked if I had a friend in Jesus.)

I beat a path between schoolyards
and the plastic debris—

                candy wrappers, playing cards,
                a Barbie's severed head—

that emerges everywhere in spring,
and certainly around townhouse projects.

A magpie cacophonic in the pine
in dialects of trills and whistles.
What was he dying to warn me about?

Your cellphone pinged
with every adulterous message,
and Love, they came quickly
and often.

The vendetta wind cuts
from the north and I am relating
too much to violence.

Nowhere to go.

Sun dodges behind late-day clouds.
I slip back into your house, surreptitiously.

What I Left in that City

Stained-glass wine goblets. Favourites
gifted from my daughter's old boyfriend.
Sacrificed because the man I was escaping—

      who insisted I not raise my eyebrows
      as the effort left lines in my forehead—

asked for the glasses to remember me by.

Christmas decorations.
Not the ones the children made—

      those treasures long gone—

but the blue and silver designer ones
that resembled emphatic rain.

My bike. Winter coats. A rolling pin.
Shelves of Canadian books
signed by friends.

A stone birdbath.
The wooden chair I assembled and painted blue.
Duvets and sheet sets. A bedroom suite,
newly purchased, and a brown couch
that wasn't quite leather.

I left several fine girlfriends.
Two plum trees and a hybrid apple:
they yielded as if that garden were Eden.

A dozen pairs of dead running shoes
dangling from garage rafters,
and a lonely two-drawer filing cabinet.
Also, one upright grand piano.

My legacy only footprints,
from the suburbs to the stars, in snow.

The Ocean Will Do That

Let Us

Let us change our names to September.
Admire bicycle seats.

Let us smile at strangers
and not appear batshit crazy.

Let us love funky architecture
and wind.

Let us notice what's important—
kites marooned in treetops,

the ins and outs of hermit crabs,
five-year-olds grateful for their thumbs.

Let us be happy in our aloneness
and appreciate gin rummy.

Let us never believe it's too cold to sit in red chairs.
Let us bow to the lowly coffee bean

and appreciate good acoustics
in narrow stairwells.

Let us take public transportation.
Give credit to cartographers

and graphic designers.
Also to the Rolling Stones.

Here's to sturdy backpacks and jackets
with skulls.

Big thanks for tiny naps,
plus crosswalks painted on busy streets.

Let us go into the woods with hearts
and pockets open,

and when we're overflowing,
let us make our winsome trails home.

Sunshine Coast Series

1.   Single pansy among stones

Yellowest ear. Stepped on rather
than around, and no sisters. Holy granite.
Saladable? Perish that fancy.

Trying so hard to be the sun it hurts.

2.   Tugboat #1

Sky apocalyptic. Spinal-ridged.
The heavens have gone reptile.

Two train cars inch-by-inch
across the Georgia Strait. And wind
currycombs the jittering pampas grass.

3.   Jellyfish

You are no salad mould. Could be. You
and six hundred siblings: rootbeer, gummy-

beared, blossoms. Larger than dinner plates.
Squelched up on the shore.

4.   Metal Fish on a stick

Monsieur Sleek.
Believes sky is the ticket: too good
for the garden's painted rocks
and ornamental autumn grass.

Nose toward Nanaimo. Tailfins blooming
rust. Air-borne.

5.   Tugboat #2

Go ahead, pull a mountain range.
Requires no effort. So what. Potash? Oilseeds?
Ain't no sleeping giant.

Captain, do you see me? Here, not waving.

6.   Himalayan Blackberries

Wine on a bush. Thimble-sized. Sacrifice
one watch, one earring. Arms. Barbed-

wire branches, and full-pail spills. Hear that?
No bear. The blue heart,
self-sustaining.

The Dead Zone

                    Dark-eyed junco
among the stalwart kiwis
on winter vines. So reserved, the sun—
brightest bird preening
through dirty conservatory windows.

Someone should wash something.

A flutterless sailboat—
white sails utterly entertaining
as it maunders
between here and what's going on
in Nanaimo.

Binoculars back to their corner, my desk
grained in cake crumbs,
unwinning lottery tickets, a hair band,
crimson-cupped tulips in decline.

Across the strait, I am the mountains,
a blue sketch. Quiet
as a rock.

They say bald eagles mate for life; a pair
in the western red cedar
                    reminding me
each time I leave the house.

Smuggler Cove Marine Provincial Park

—For Flo

She says be careful it's slippery and I ask fir or cedar and she says oysters and don't you love the way moss drips like that and oh yes I definitely do.

She's been to San Francisco fourteen times and I'm losing sleep because my son's flying in with his girlfriend and maybe if Mark owned a tight pair of Levis he'd be hot and whoa close call on that cliff.

We squeeze past three hikers to gawk at Thormanby Island and just around the bend there's a great beach and let's go to the city for plastic surgery consults and the girlfriend's from Germany.

After Chinese immigrants built the Canadian Pacific Railway William Kelly smuggled them to the US for a buck a head and evaded arrest by hiding in the cove and I need a hat plus her boy dancing at the Gay Pride Parade.

She says no more roller derby and I wonder if my son's in love and February in Saskatchewan was never like this arbutus.

I can't read the minute directions on the $50 can of bear spray and she's pierced three cocks and can't read it either and wouldn't it be just our luck to be doomed in the wilds by nearsightedness.

Yes to a little lipo beneath the chin and eyelids for sure and her daughter's pregnant and we met in a beach bar in Indonesia and what kind of duck is that.

Rum-rummers used the cove to store bootleg and the German gal's a cobbler and don't spray downwind and what if she hates me and Scarlett if it's a girl and another Monday morning hike is done.

The Heart is a Red Umbrella

1.
Opening, closing, rained upon
and blown inside out.

2.
Vancouver morning. We brunched
at an Indian bistro. Outside, a parade
of sopping umbrellas:

> grim black grazing pink polka dots.
> Monet's garden
> rib-to-rib with a navy CBC,
> an impervious yellow tulip,
> Burberry tartan, and all God's animals
> running riot from the ark.

3.
I would leave him; he always knew it.

4.
A strapping rain on Robson, and us
with our curry and commentary.

The most enjoyable brunch I've ever had,
the man I loved then said.

5.
Twelve years dissolve like salt in water.

Does he also fill his doorway at night
and rust beneath the dripping stars?

Five Day Visit

After my mother leaves I want you
to fuck me like *Australopithecus*
in the sheets that held her—
remarkably luminous—
in our rented beach house.

The ocean will do that. Little girl
she became, tipsy
over the egg-sized stones,
pocketing clam shells, washing them
in Palmolive dish soap

beneath razoring wind and bald eagles.
For what? To line the sill
above her Saskatchewan sink. To touch
when winter's meanest and it's dangerous
even to breathe.

Her last morning we rested
on a bench marking a stranger's death.
All day these altars for the dead: lily bouquet
folded in its cone of flower-shop paper:
We're not leaving you behind, Dearest Frank,

we're taking you with us.
Four white-painted tricycles below a steep driveway.
Lion's mane jellyfish dying in the sand.
We sat like interlopers in the harsh sunlight
and watched Harlequin ducks

move like a current—I want to say *umbilically*—
into the Salish Sea. Pools in whale-coloured rocks
and we had forgotten cameras.
She was concerned she'd be late for the bus
to the ferry, to the airport, home.

Now I fill the bowl of wine.
Hallowe'en, but no kids at the door.

My mother is off with her bags like Mary Poppins,
off with her worries and four slices of cheese
wrapped in plastic and tucked inside her purse.

Her washed shells forgotten
on the patio table. Ravage me. For now,
and for that future hour
when a sister will call to say *Mom's gone.*
And I will not be prepared.

I Wait for an Epiphany and Don't Expect a Bright Light

Places

After a few drinks someone brings up Las Vegas and who has been
there and you have not and you've just got to go and it's not about
the gambling or the shows and then onto New York and the crime
that you've never experienced MOMA or Central Park or even
hailing a cab like Carrie in "Sex and the City" and don't some places
exceed expectations like London and Paris and who knew Montreal
would feel so good to walk around in at night and Cirque de Soleil
but not Celine Dion and zero interest in LA but what if we made a
map for the rest of our lives and we couldn't die until we'd hit like
our top five destinations but there's that cartel business in Mexico
and maybe Moscow or Gdańsk and it's perpetually cool to include
Nepal and what about the Florida Keys and anyone done Denver or
walking across Scotland and Thailand's ever-popular and certainly
Argentina or possibly Oktoberfest and don't be such a tourist but
Greece for the white-washed towns then back to Las Vegas and
you say to sit on the edge of the Grand Canyon and feel tiny and
someone says *ant* and you say *no way, tinier.*

Rue de Menoncourt: Notes on a Global Home Exchange

The house opens in many directions. I lounge on the terrace, bare
legs tendered to the sun like I'm fifteen, home from school, slathered
in baby oil and believing a tan will improve my gladness. No one
spoke of skin cancer, of aging, of how forty years ahead the left side
of my face would confetti in brown spots and I'd yelp at my own
reflection.

First week of relaxation in two years and the fallout from our teary
quarrels (concerning roundabouts and my aptitude for wrong
directions) is a kind of tintinnabulation, but I'm convinced we hate
each other a pinch less today.

Time hangs like a piano-struck note. Heat like my Saskatchewan
childhood. Flies whirlpool in windows. You don only underwear and
buses pass with the regularity of clouds.

All villages should ring with church bells at improbable hours.

An apple-sized pressure to do something—*Mon Dieu*, it's France—
but I can't magic the energy to dawdle through church tombstones
and touch the concrete shoulders of the dead, can't figure how far we
are from Dijon.

One sprawling month in this red-doored elegance. Ubiquitous white
lace over paned-glass windows, and aerial maps directing our gaze
on the walls.

We eat no end of croissants. You run out of my sight down the tree-
lined lanes, and our socks bake into crêpes on the clothesline.

Impossibly, my French regresses.

Missing Exits

Then I collapse
and press my face into the very floor of France.

Ants, and mossy clover. Sun a pallid thumbtack
over Eglise Notre-Dame de L'Assomption.

A bean-stalk maple to shade, and the *n'importe où*
of a lawn mower, plus birds

to mitigate the highways behind us.
Neighbors beyond the cedar-hedge

converse in floral rhythms.
Cars in the rush-hour from Basel

or Mulhouse. Phaffans' church bell percussions
over the luster of fields

as it has since 1724.
Tomorrow I'll walk to Roppe for croissants

while you make the coffee. I will try again
not to go blind

at the table, so transfixed by the smoky plume
that never waivers

where the fields meet the Vosges Mountains.
I will pin your beach towel to the line

and appreciate the way books intrinsically know
how to be quiet and to beckon.

I have devoured villages of Swiss chocolate,
and soon I'll start on the wine.

But this is the hour to stay lowdown and watchful.
A brigade of ants

circumnavigates the tree's base—
hollow to hollow—cartoonish

crossings over and beneath brethren.
I feel close to something. These ants:

Napoleonic in purpose, as if each knows
exactly what's to be done.

Porrentruy

The lipstick of windows: flowers
in fire-colours
beneath black-louvered shutters.

Switzerland, I want to fall in love
with our fifth day on vacation,
but we're on the wrong highway
in a borrowed grey Cadillac
that's making sounds
like someone learning to play alphorn.

Mountain tunnels become draconic throats
and go on for indecent lengths.
BMWs torpedo past
and I fear a death like Diana's—

                    in a foreign country,
                    and decades too young.

The sky is a low metal breastplate
and I fail magnificently as navigator.
All the slowing for round-a-bouts
and my partner's fountains of rage
feed our alpine silence: for a time
we inadvertently cross into France.

Switzerland, I apologize.
                We are beasts.

Your red and orange blossoms froth
romantically from window-boxes
with shutters like muttonchops;
your green valleys compel me
to shepherd anything with a bell.

We spy a sign for a castle in Porrentruy,
scan for turrets above burgher houses
through the windshield's pox of rain.

Hello, cobblestones. Hello medieval steps
and fortifications, stained glass
and gothic ramparts. How silly I feel
feeling anything but reverence
in the presence of Réfous Tower,
standing since 1271.

This is my first castle, my partner whispers
in boy-voice, and I soften,
but it's too late
to lower the drawbridge between us.

Can't Write Today

Because I'm not in a Mexican hammock slung beneath a spruce
tree chorused in brown birds.
Because of last night's thunder, sky flashing in sheets and a
tap-steady rain between the bedroom and bathroom walls.
Because of an unfulfilled promise of tennis.
Because of the warrior cockroach who surprised us in the stairwell
of the Lisbon apartment.
Because of contemporary art.
Because of your hideous toenails.
Because of the dropped ring scams near the Musée d'Orsay.
Because we learned to scream *Nyet!*
Because there may always be tornadoes.
Because of mean bus drivers.
Because of blind beggars with dogs on the Charles Bridge.
Because of the Eiffel Tower as golden torch when viewed at night
from a boat after a Fat Bikes cycling tour.
Because of the Brazilian who blamed me for her crash.
Because of the sound my feet made on the hardwood floors
in the Egon Schiele Gallery in Český Krumlov.
Because my little brother is memory now.
Because of BB King.
Because we were told *It is not possible!* at a sex club in Prague.
Because we met Rick Steves in the I.P. Pavlova metro station
and his grandparents homesteaded in Edmonton.
Because of grapes and Alsatian towns.
Because of a thirty-kilometre hike with a sixty-two-year-old
Dane named Sigrun.
Because I called her *Sigrid* until I knew better.
Because of swans and covered bridges in Lucerne.
Because of funiculars and the palace Michael Jackson wished to buy.
Because of cheese and sausages in a Freiburg market.
Because James Gandolfini died too.
Because I don't speak to anyone.
Because of flipflops up to and all the way through the
Haut-Kœnigsbourg Castle.

Because of the bitchy Tourist Information woman in Belfort.
Because three times you couldn't remember your VISA password
at a cash register and lost the privilege of charging.
Because of the near-arrest in Estoril and the sirens sounded like
WW2 inside the cop car speeding toward Lisbon.
Because of those hard plastic seats.
Because you wouldn't tell me why.
Because I needed to laugh and you snapped at me for covert
photography.
Because of a dozen postcards I never sent.
Because of too much running to nowhere in the highest heat.
Because of the legend of The Cock of Barcelos.
Because of peacocks and their five chicks at home in an artfully-
designed B & B.
Because of being too tired to go to the bullfight.
Because of Strasbourg.
Because I came in a whirlpool at Baden-Baden.
Because of Prague's cheap beer.
Because *L'addition* is cool to say in a restaurant.
Because of striking Swiss Air workers.
Because of this Humboldt Motors Body Shop pen.
Because of jet lag.
Because of Monday.
Because of radio commercials.
Because of Portuguese oysters that travel to France before returning
to Portugal to be sold at ten times the price.
Because I'm too old to fit in at art school.
Because of *pastéis de nata*.
Because a woman with hands protruding from her shoulders
handled her cigarettes with finesse.

Alfama

The Moors left cobbled snake trails
and all day you weather them
believing Lisbon might be your destiny.
You are seduced by bread and olives,
by the legend of Barcelos
and decanters of cheap white wine.

Apartments gleam like buttons
in the all-day sun, as if boasting—
                    the earthquake did not claim us.
Pastries burst into feathers on your tongue.

Coal-eyed children
wobble over stones on rust-blistered bikes.
You imagine learning to walk here.
You imagine falling into the spell
of blue-green tiles and beach-light.

You eat standing in the street, alone,
and it is almost Africa. There are almonds.
Tin-roofed shanties beneath train tracks,
a folded crone in cathedral-shadows.

Your blouses and under-things surrender
out the window; black panties butterfly
                    to the balcony below.

Night shakes its cape and suddenly
lanes choke with grilled fish and drunks
glow amber. Patrons crowd entries
to basement Fado clubs and laments smoke
into the long-throated lanes. You think
of hungry, wide-winged birds.
Port-coloured stains. The red petals
whisked from window-boxes, crushed
beneath sandals and stilettos.
Keep your back to the wall.

The waiter brings a blanket for bare shoulders.
I could see you, he says, *shivering.*

Salema

1.
White wine, white linens, white architecture.
Grapes in bee-hived bunches.

Even the wind here: white.

2.
Catholic Mass in the fishermen's shack;
coffee-row in the daytime.
Latin music swells from the patio bar
and church ladies hawk pastries and brandy
to people like me
while a parade of rainbow-flagged boats
floats parishioners over the turquoise sea
to sing some kind of praises,
and no bells ring.

3.
Coastline: a litany
of "From Here to Eternity" beaches.

On my back in the sand, head inside a cave
of toppled boulders. Panty-exposed
and all of me feels
                    like fire-sticks.

Can't take it
a wave-break longer.

4.
A morning hike
following roads I don't know
which lead to trails
and always to guesses. Barking dogs
and pear trees. Almonds and figs.
A Roman road, 2000 years old.

A sign says *Figueira Fort* and snakes
rattle the grasses. I wait
for an epiphany and don't expect
a bright light.

Crawl up a cliff, leave some skin
among the brambles. Pee at the summit
like the boy I must be.

Capes and coves
and flaking red cliff-faces
to all the tumble-way down.
Someone has painted a happy face
on a cactus that appears to have ears.

5.
Not far away, Cape Sagres.
                    Oyster fishermen.
                    Cabo de St. Vicente.
Holy "Age of Discovery." Soon I will know
they sell postcards
and hippie dresses
at the veritable end of the world.

Church where Vasco da Gama prayed
before setting sail: blessedly—
no gift shop.

6.
Half a half-litre left,
alone and facing a plum-faced cigar smoker
with a monumental gold ring.

7.
I am in sudden love
with the women in floppy sunhats.
And the unabashed ones, topless,
playing a ball-batting game.
The two-year-olds on inflatable circus animals,
unaware of how heartily the sea wants to eat them.
Also the Portuguese mister with warm eyes
who stroked the length of my arm
perfectly, and just once—
                    more people should do that more often.

And love for the couples
who don't speak over swordfish
and lemons they do not finish.

The fishing boats. Sailboats in the distance,
no bigger than folded serviettes.
White, of course. Like the relentless wind,
and spanking new skin.

8.
Of the epiphany, only this:
Buy good hiking boots.

9.
I asked the bartender for a paper placemat
so I could scribble this down.
                    First one became a kite.
This is the second one.

What I Like About You

Reno Air Races

Flew into night-time Nevada.
Star-spangled valley: sky top-side down.
You parked your sexy plane;
I fit the plug in the Pitot tube,
set wooden blocks
to jar the Mooney Ovation's wheels.
The rental car waiting like a steed.

—

No night and day inside the hotel's casino
where I practised my habit
of searching for familiar eyes
within storm clouds of strangers
and you did not win at Blackjack,
though we pretended
I brought intermittent luck.

—

You had a billionaire to meet at breakfast.
I ran downtown in a ponytail
past sex shops
and back-pack-wearing crackheads
on low-slung bikes.
Went for the special at McDonald's, like a local
or a low-income poet.

—

I don't believe in paying for parking
so we walked a mile in scorpion heat,
bought two cans of Coke Zero
from tweens hawking it
like last century's lemonade
in the dust of a roadside stand.

Commissionaires checked my purse at the ticket gate.

I took close-up photos of grown men
in shirts graphic with airplanes and sweat stains,
you flirted with a stripper
selling calendars—Shannon's Cannons: July.

—

B-51 Mustangs, F4U-4 Corsair fighters, Sea Furies.

—

I melted into your thigh by degrees
while planes shot over hills
and tricked around pylons
with elegant ferocity.
Learned about bank turns and your lust
for flight, how pilots and spectators
can crumble into stamp-sized bits of ash.

The scene smelled like burritos and sunblock,
like a situation rapidly becoming familiar.

—

The F-22 Raptor made me consider
killing machines, the disparate men—
        geniuses and musicologists, inventors and kiteboarders—
I find myself spiralling towards earth with.

This damn heart.
This damn heart.
This damn heart in flames.

Oarlocks

After-scent of sex, coffee
and four fried eggs.

Left the raft's feeble safety again.
Shallow-dived into that brine of chemistry:

welcome bronze current of thighs, raw anatomy. I kiss
your eyes as you raft rivers in sleep,

hold your hand on the pillow like it's fragile.
Think of fossils, trilobites.

We get to splash in this country awhile
and it's all apple gardens

and Facebook photos that boast
cells snapping alive like minnows.

I can swim as well as anyone
through the archaeology

of limestone caves and canyons.
But I always enthuse too large.

Call it a heart condition, mine
quite Pacific: I can't even guess where we'll sink.

Still: joy from sediment to soul—
         if you *believe* in that chimera.

This goddamn flotilla of atoms
gets stirred up, sets me sun-side—

I moult
into an industry of hope.

So let's be oceanic. In time,
the moon will need its own dark way again.

We stand in the raft
and forget to secure oarlocks.

The river swallows homes, and families
slide down the eroding banks.

This does not require philosophers.
We're briefly swollen with hormones.

Let's knot these ropes into something
wet and slippery and breathing.

Hottest July on Record

A marten in a tree near the suspension bridge—
you almost cooed it down.

You have this way with animals
and the muscular rivers
where you're most alive in your skin.

What is it like to be so solemn
wild things are drawn to your shadows?

That summer we tracked
a dozen red suns descending
into the restless Pacific.
Washington, Oregon, California.
My desire to touch you
was palpable and unreciprocated:
the landscape I learned best
was your back.

Later, your cottage, the crepuscular hours.
Loons scored the cold lake and forest smoke
blurred time because it buried the sun
we grew up with. Bears
paid me more attention than you did.

Back in my bed on Vancouver island,
your pouting a counterpoint
to my surreptitious burning.
Brought you freshly-picked blackberries,
my arms still bleeding,
fingertips porcupined with thorns.

Tsawwassen

To be of this bone-thinning decade
and a blur of limbs
on a tandem bike
behind the aerodynamic helmet
of an online-met man
I know far less
than the mystery of Vancouver.

Oceanside trail, lungs and hair flaming
past country homes veiled
beneath blizzards of lilacs
and exuding the tenor of nostalgia—
porch swings
and wrap-around verandahs.

I've been drunk with months of solitude,
little more than equipment,
and soon we're riding through fields
plowed but unplanted—
                            a college of hours and places
never dreamt of on wishbones.

Where do you want to be in a year?
this near stranger asks.

Here, in Boundary Bay,
where seals practise surprises.
Here, in this pedal-pushing light.

Lopsided

At Beach Grove
I hold your arm amid red crab shells
and Sunday cyclists wearing mittens.
I'm elated with blackberry brambles
and strangers volunteering hellos
while salt and pepper snow geese
write a script above root-churned fields,
soon to grow ever more shopping malls.

I'm too-clearly invested
and you are *Stalled on many fronts,*
say: *This feels lopsided.*

We digress to starlings—
you remember the word *murmuring* first.

I aim my camera at the January sky—
my fool lens again
making too much of creatures
and North Shore mountaintops.

—

On a dark road
to the ferry terminal
after your confession: you cannot love me.

It's okay, I said. *This happens all the time.*

I kissed you, held you
through the purgatory of hours.

Sleep wouldn't rescue me
so I gathered my bags
and bed-side pink panties
at 3:30 a.m., attempted to leave discretely
as moonlight.

When I drove away from your bed,
the air smelled of irony
and bougainvillea.

—

On the ferry with a purple pillow,
hood pulled over my eyes
like a teenaged boy.

Is it hard for your kind, dropping
your crushing bombs
on couches, over phones, in brief texts
with emoticons?

The captain warns of a breathing sea
and blasts the ferry's horn.
I cry softly
against the vibrating window.

The ocean knows something
about being a woman.

Perseids

You say all that's been getting you through
is the thought of lying in a dark field with me
beneath what we might glean of the universe,
maybe catch the meteor show.

I say Okay, and we throw two cans of beer
and a blanket into the cab, jump the fence
at the soccer pitch to lie on artificial turf.

Briefly lovers, we've transitioned into friends,
and what I like about you is how you talk
about the very soil of life, this circumference
of fear we exist within.

I say I adore how inconsequential
a night sky makes one feel.

You say your neck's been killing you
since you were slammed at an intersection,
and what do I want for the rest of my life?

Above us, the light-bazaar.

You reach for my hand and we cluster
stars into new constellations—

                    a flying squirrel,
                    a fan rake.

Between meteors, the less spectacular satellites
and airplanes, possibly
spearing toward Iceland.

You speak of recent failures, the whiplash
of vitriolic texts.

I've committed to someone distant
as asteroids.

For minutes, nothing but night birds
that mimic wailing cats.
We crush
the matching aluminum cans.

You can't kiss me, I say,
but we can talk about anything.

After Tony Hoagland's "Reasons to Survive November"

After the party last night I came home with the leftovers
and ate the sushi and fancy cheeses *tout de suite*,
though I didn't have any crackers, just fingers
to scoop those mottled clumps
that resembled diseases
straight into the augur of my throat.
Wasn't even hungry. And after, I didn't sleep.

This morning I forced myself into the light rain
wearing blue plastic pants over my pajamas.
I walked deep into the forest and took photos of things
that usually make me happy to be alive—
        or, in the case of the creek's dead salmon,
grateful to be human.

                    It's not depression.
Hell, as a rule
I'm so upbeat I piss others off,
but today melancholy followed me
like a sharp-clawed animal
through the cedars and ivy-scarved trees.

Tony, it's not even November that gets me.
It's that November neighbours December, month of brothers
who died too young, terrible season of Christmas—
which hasn't been fun since at least 2005
(and has never been affordable).

It's awful to feel this way when I have two good legs
and someone who loves me.
Today all I managed for him
was an egg salad sandwich.
He also got the leftover apple pie
I took to last night's housewarming, and few people tried.
I picked those apples and made that crust.

Seems a lot of my friends are giving up food these days,
like I've given up wine, though I keep some red fire
in the cabinet in case of earthquake
or the other kinds of disasters I attract.

Soon this day will close and I'll crawl
into the back bedroom's cave. I'll grow too warm
in this ridiculous flannel onesie (with pink unicorns)
I got for a buck, shuck it off
then bloody well freeze.

December like a gauntlet.
Christmas: an annual trial.
And you, fine poet, now you're gone, too.

Tony, I'm going to wake tomorrow, *shove joy like a knife*
into my own heart over and over
and force myself toward pleasure.

Your poem on my fridge once again,
counselling through the year's harsh wet end.

Late December

You migrate toward coffee shops
for the velvet of human voices, the warmth
of an oversized mug and indie music.

You are certain no one sees you
falling in love
with the scrape of a chair,
the drooping cedar wreath
in the Beantime's window.

The white-grey sky is a pelt. Raindrops on glass
a bead you're tempted to trace
with your tongue.

Across the street:

    Fox and Hounds.
    A gym.
    Women in designer rubber boots.

Everything is exquisite
but once again, no plans for New Year's Eve.

Getting to be a long time;
you'd like to hold anyone's hand.

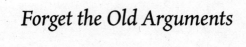

Forget the Old Arguments

Forget the Old Arguments

They don't matter any longer.
The world is ending. You're right,
it always has been, but now we can smell it
curling at the edges, love letter
over the orange eraser of flame.

Forests are burning: the environmentalists
had it right. The sky's milky
with smoke and despair.
Bears and cougars meander
through our carports.
Like the movies, something big
is going down.

But miracles still happen:
tumours disappear,
children are dug from the roulette
of earthquakes, bombed buildings.
Wisteria is dripping from trees
all over town; I can't be the only one
saying: *Holy fuck … look at those trees!*

Yesterday I raced around Holland Creek Trail
after a blackberry smoothie.
The black bear saw me
the moment I saw him. Only one path,
so we shared it.

After Ross Gay's "To the Fig Tree on 9ᵗʰ and Christian"

Because I'm awake before 5:00 a.m. for no good reason, I find you,
Ross Gay, on a podcast. Your mind's a rose garden. You write like
someone who truly *gets* the universe, and throws his whole life into
his work.

A few things are falling apart in my own tiny world. My toilets need
replacing. I must do yoga for my miserable back. More blackberries
are ready to be picked and I've got to get out there, though it's
simmering, the sun prickly, and my limbs already resemble games of
X's and O's.

I can't seem to catch up with my life, but love's found me again: the
mist below the mountain's no longer a painting of my heart.
I kayak, hike, cycle. I grow kale and friendships. I've had vaccines.
And I've never had to swim through the night to escape my own
country.

Catalogue of Unabashed Gratitude. Ross, the title alone's worth the
price. I order online: how long before your poetry comes from
Blackwell's in England? Days or weeks, one distant morning it'll
arrive like unexpected flowers—orange, or yellow. I'll throw my
whole self into it. Pages like petals. I'll touch them like skin.

Ladysmith: Gratitude 1

Any morning that begins with Tai Chi
on a marina dock is fine by me.
But what do I know?

Only that we are red poppies
for the ambrosial breeze and the moored boats
pay no attention; they exist

only to counterpoint
the ocean's blue scholarship,
the arrow shapes of trees

that ascend the mountain we face—
    where I live calmly
with few things

in a tall white box. Today:
pewter clouds grasp the bird's tail.
The white crane flaps its wings.

Ladysmith: Gratitude 2

I run to the marina to be mesmerized
by jellyfish, and to forget

I may forever come home
to an empty house.

There is Syria and violence,
hunger and political scandal,

and I do nothing about these matters,
captivated by my petty griefs.

Eighteen visceral months
since a man's professed love,

and me with my pathetic need
to hold another warm hand,

to be whispered to across a pillow.
I have no commerce, no potentiality.

Fridge bare but for dead-fallen apples
donated by friends.

And who could understand this planet
of no small desire,

or the joy found in valentines
masquerading as maple leaves.

Easy to blind facts; I must remind myself:
even the ragged moments are beautiful.

Ladysmith: Gratitude 3

All you need to know about me is spring-melt.
Is moss embellishing stone and the great fallen firs.
Is sun's velvet glove, equally generous on my face,
the thriving salal, rust-red arbutus.

I've fallen in love with the world again.
From Rotary Hill, my little town
is a fairytale told in white squares
and school yards. Beyond it, the blue-eyed harbour,
then Yellow Point Peninsula (undeniably green),
and the Salish Sea,
where a ferry's doing its important work.

When I walk in the rare snow I know I'm born of prairie,
but the Steller's jays have adopted me. Crocuses,
so damn earnest I could weep.

And when others notice me—the larger animals,
those who might walk dogs in the deeper woods—
can they know my heart's exploding?

I want you here. Leave everything behind.
Mountain water in the cups of our palms,
and nothing else to need.

Ladysmith: Gratitude 4

The southeast sun was a bonfire
and a bald eagle
knew exactly where she should be.

Dogs were taking masters for walks. I smiled
at drivers and said hello to backpack-wearing teens
trudging toward their institution. A dozen doves

exploded off a powerline. The ocean
was a bronze wedge between house shapes.
There were roses, still on the vine. In November.

At the beach I was alone and the waves were plucky.
I sat on a wet cedar log, studied stones
and maple leaves; a distant island

was a reclining woman in grey-blue silhouette.
(There the shoulders, there the hips.)
A pleasure-craft mutely motored through the harbour.

A breakaway log bobbed in the water
and was not a seal.
I inhaled cedar and oyster scents.

A lone seagull squawked
at Transfer Beach Park,
and I just stayed there, solitarily, sparking.

May

The sky is weeping in a soft way, as one does
when heartache's become old.

We are so many weeks into this
        pandemic, and each other.

On the balcony
        I power-washed last week—

the camellia keeps dropping pink blossoms
I float in blue pottery bowls.

Small bits of beauty.
All I'm seeking during these days

we did not know were coming.
These months of ridiculous chores.

You're in Toronto to care for your mother
who confuses day for night, Canada for Trinidad,

and calls you by your Chinese name.
I still hardly know you.

Our first kisses at the coulee
while the world was already changing.

The daffodils, magnolias, the cherry trees—
        clearly, they did not know either.

The Quiet

So pronounced it takes a shape. It desires
the syllables of a name.

On Saturday night streets,
in this white-walled townhouse

punctuated by a red couch
like a garish smear of lipstick

against the north wall:
silence.

This non-sound the definition of time
invisibly rolling forward

against future shores.
Yes, the creek still sings

its silver song, and at 7:00 pm
my neighbours ritualistically ring bells

and the firehall siren clears the air
with its salute to healthcare workers,

but then it's back to the inflamed quiet.
Perhaps a check-in with the news,

though now every other tragedy
is made so much worse

because of the collective backdrop.
It's getting dangerous to breathe.

Don't get me wrong: I'm not unhappy,
but I have become superstitious

not tempting fate with even a thought
toward when a vaccine might blossom.

And I'm cautious, going back to the old ways:
hiding rolls of money in the house,

towering canned food
in the basement

beside the camping gear
I am not using.

Surreptitiously preparing, in case of anarchy,
a bloodbath—

              I should not have said that.
I must be a quiet house

in this mute and quivering sci-fi movie
we're all trying to reach the end of.

The soundtrack is silence
and it's disconcerting, foreign—

like casualty numbers in Africa,
like mysteries we may never pronounce.

Thanksgiving 2020

Roses at their ultimate in October,
the hopscotch play of light

on the blackberried path toward the beach.
A blue kite harboured in an oak tree

and the two—wait, *three*—crows conversing
between the circuitry of branches. The wind

blows through me on a park bench
beside a zinnia the size of my face.

Some days I almost feel young.
True, these are strange times,

but there's a dollop of honey in most days:
the librarian said, *Enjoy the book,*

it's a good one, and I've been kayaking
around small Gulf Islands. Let's not even talk

about all the apples ripening around the house,
or having time to pick up my old guitar.

It's two-for-one punchcard day
at the coffee shop where I review books

on the often-empty second floor
and watch cars navigate the roundabout.

I float down First Avenue with a rare feeling—
        I am part of the fabric

with my take-away Americano,
my thrift store leggings and ball cap.

The metronome of my life's cranked right down.
I keep company with the creek's spawning salmon,

am closer to reading the books
that turtle up my stairs.

Another truth: I've never needed much
from factories, but give me slow boats of sunlight

across the water, across the floor,
or the white noise of rain

as a sleep aid. The flowers inside flowers
that are roses. Robin-song—that brightest refrain.

Christmas Prayer

God of details in a maidenhair fern.
God in the dewdrop at the end of a pine needle.
God in tiny tree frogs with mighty voices.
God in the silver of bark lichen.
God in mud, and disobedient dogs.
God in the tealight candle's precarious flame
at a Blue Christmas service,
and in the hands of the wet-eyed
man or woman barely managing
one narrow breath after the next.
God of our too-soon gone.
God in cedars. In squirrels.
God of symbiosis.
God of our mistakes.
God in the sun burnishing rock and creek.
God in trails smothered in maple leaves.
God in slippery bridges.
God in equally slippery slugs.
God in so many waterfalls.
God of grace after failure.
God in new calendars.
God in parting clouds.
God in knitting bones.
God in the understory.
God in both seagull and eagle.
God in you.
God in me.

How To Love Your Life

Begin in the woods. Feel the tree-breeze cool
your limbs and listen to the soundscape
change to creek-song, birdness. Chew salal berries.
Press your palms on the pelts of moss, sit
across from a waterfall called Crystal.

Spend hours reading beside a café window
with a Goliath cup of coffee, a slim glass of water
that tastes like good fortune.

From time to time, look up:
trios of thirteen-year-old girls
with legs long as horses'.
An incoherent man wearing a blue guitar.

Walk alone through the busy downtown streets
and know the answers
when strangers ask for directions.
Admire gladiolus. Admire the social hive
that's a small-town post office.

Hike through a tunnel to a beach
and note the perfection of kayaks, smooth swimmers,
and dripping ice cream cones:
mint chocolate chip, strawberry.
The playground's pulsing with acrobatic children
thinking no further than now.

The present is salmonberries.
The present: bald eagles.
The present is the only page we have.

Manitoulin Suite

Manitoulin Suite

—For Peter

1.
Sun-bleached sugar shacks, milkweed,
and monarch butterflies.

My palm sinks into a pillow of tree moss
and you explain how sugar's tapped
from maples in the hundred-acre woods.

We walk hand-in-hand and for hours
in sopping shoes through birch-light, crow-song.
You show me erratics, hunting blinds,
and the rock you'd have lunch on
with your son enroute to town
for double ice cream cones.

Generational stories, preserved
in these northern Ontario woods
since you were a boy
learning to play violin like your Bulgarian father—
the gentle gardener, long buried
beneath cedars in Sudbury.

I've come to your cottage in the tall shadow
of your wife who died too soon
and find the anticipated museum of your lives:
the kids' lifejackets and Archie comics;
her badminton racquet, jackets, her bike
which I ride through the pastoral countryside
between a corridor of birdsong.

I can lower the seat if you need me to, you said,
before we pedaled toward Mindemoya.
No thanks, it's just right, I told you.

A white lie, small as a bellflower.

2.
Days of rain and almost-rain.

We forget the well-travelled laundry
on the line, and now it droops
across chairs around the cottage
like guests who won't go home
after you're all talked out
and desperate for the refuge of nothingness.

I find you sullen on the couch
beneath the frayed curtains, treading
in ghosts and reverie.

How could you not? Everything possesses
a history here, from your mother's
vintage Austrian teapot—turquoise
with stars, like Lake Mindemoya—
to the beachball, deflating for decades
and affectionately called Caillou.

In the first week: one sunny day,
a single swim between the floating dock
and the farthest buoy, both of us dizzy
from the effort, from the velocity
of radical changes in these parallel lives
we've experienced as obsessive runners
and pathological workers, cities apart
with our long marriages and two kids each.

You kiss me with your wet mouth
and I don't give a damn about the sun
making me even older.

3.
Four thousand four hundred miles.
Pandemic anxieties, a series of stops and highways,
one dead bear, and the top of Lake Superior
to twist a key into the cottage lock.

There's work to do. Cloud-bound cedars
your parents transplanted from ditches
on Ketchankookem Road
dwarf the cottage your father built,
and we are days sawing and lopping,
clearing the understory.

We drive the truck into town
for groceries, lumber, wi-fi and beer.
Catch 'em and cook 'em, I say,
the most obvious joke
as we cruise past the sign.

4.
 I want to hang the hammock near the pear tree
then somewhere else, because I believe
in chasing down the light
and revere spontaneity. I hope
to fold up here with pen and notebook.
I'll let the midday sun become
what matters, slide into the inspirational
company of thrushes and squirrels.

Eventually, two small chickadees
court on a cedar bough
like I'm not even there.

5.
It doesn't feel the same.

You mean the island, the community.
You mean this place you've inherited.

Consequence of the dual trains of time and change,
the mountainous beauty of your reinvention
on Vancouver Island.

Should you sell the cottage?

The riding mower won't start.
The water pressure tank leaks.
The tool shed's a disaster.
Mouse nest in the barbecue.
Covid's closed businesses.
Real estate's at an all-time high.
The weather's been grim.
The woods are encroaching.
Even CBC comes in crackly on the radio.

And where the hell are the cardinals
you promised me?

You're *not ready yet*, but summon the gusto
to begin pruning the deep-rooted knickknacks
and spare bedding. I hold open the bags,
note the blue-and-white checked squares
on the quilt your mother stitched
match the fabric of her house-dress apron.

That's my mother, you say.
She never wasted a thing.

6.
Lightness comes, and I fear everything
is a dream. I run to the window
when you're building the new shed
to be certain you are real.

Even with my injured foot,
we play a tennis match. You beat me
at checkers over morning coffee. Always
so much petitions our attention: the guitars,
hiking trails, books we've brought
to read aloud to each other
from the east and west ends of the couch.

Skin.

We make love in the late afternoons.
Breezes plume the sheers
above our temples
and redistribute the humidity and light.

You dream of your old black lab, Zack, a rescue
with half an ear. *He was so happy*
to see me, you say. *I had no idea*
why he was here.

7.
A second day of sunshine.

We pump the bike tires and ride south,
out of town, past the closed school
and the grocery store
where pandemic protocols
are adhered to: we're not allowed
to enter together.

We cycle to the cemetery,
make a game of finding the oldest grave
among the Anglo-Saxon names. There,
by the maple: *Frank Gordon, Beloved Son
of Andrew and Martha Gordon, died
June 4th, 1883, Aged 21 years.*

What's always on the tip of my tongue:
You found me.

We stand there, perspiring, touching.
Sharing what's left in the water bottle.

I think it's already tomorrow, you say.
A small poem, irrefutably true.

Notes and Acknowledgements

The poems within this book score a long season in my life defined by radical changes—in partners, provinces, jobs—and several pieces allude to acute loneliness, but they also, I hope, illustrate my perpetual love affair with wonder and the natural world, and reflect how one can fashion a full and rich life with surprisingly simple pleasures.

I appreciate those who've supported me as I ever-so-slowly continue learning where, and with whom, I belong. Peter Mutafov, you hiked and kayaked into my life at precisely the right hour—you're my forest. Tom Renton, exceptional neighbour and friend, you were a balm each time I was in pieces, and I must owe you a little lifetime in meals. Helen Herr, thanks for being my biggest fan and an extraordinary mother. Flo Bevan, we've been kicking up trouble together since my Sechelt days. Anna Marie Sewell, how I miss our weekly singing and guitar-playing in Edmonton. Rachel Dunstan Muller, thanks for the walk-and-talks in and around Ladysmith; and Dianne Rudolf, cheers to you for Big Hike Mondays and other shenanigans. Taylor Leedahl and Logan Leedahl, so much gratitude to you both for growing up with me and making it so fun and easy to be your mother.

My gracious and insightful editor, Donna Kane, you helped me sweep out the dust and polish the stones, and I so enjoyed the process. Debra Bell, thank you for giving me radiant news on New Year's Eve 2020. Kimberly Kiel, your "Scenic Route to Alaska" is sublime and I'm so glad it graces the cover of this collection. Hearty thanks to the entire crew at Radiant Press: Debra Bell, John Kennedy, Tania Wolk, Mia Bell, and thanks also to publicist Nathaniel Moore.

Earlier incarnations of some of these poems previously appeared in journals and anthologies. I'm thankful to the editors and publishers for giving these works their debut.

—

"The Quiet" appeared in *We Are One: Poems from the Pandemic* (Bayeux Press) in 2020

"Single Pansy Among Stones" (included in "Sunshine Coast Series") was published in *The Best Canadian Poetry in English*, 2013 (Tightrope Books, editors Sue Goyette and Molly Peacock), and in *The Best of the Best Canadian Poetry in English* (Tightrope Books, editors Molly Peacock and Anita Lahey), 2017

"Upon Meeting Owen Wilson in an Organic Grocery Store" was published under a longer title in *I Found It at the Movies: An Anthology of Film Poems* edited by Ruth Roach Pierson (Guernica Editions, 2014)

"Ways to Be Happier" was originally titled "To a Grandchild, Not Yet Conceived" and published in The Society, Spring 2014

"The Pantry of All There Is" was published in Freefall Magazine, Volume XXIV Number 1, Winter 2014

"Himalayan Blackberries" and "Single Pansy Among Stones" ("Sunshine Coast Series") were published in Contemporary Verse 2, Volume 35, Issue 2, Fall 2012

"Song for the Homeless as We Drive to Ruth's Chris Steak House in a Red Convertible on a Thursday Night in June" appeared in *Modern Morsels: Selections of Short Fiction and Poetry* (McGaw-Hill Ryerson) 2012

—

"Aflama" – Shortlisted for Arc's "Poem-of-the-Year" Contest 2014

"Deluge" – Shortlisted for Arc's "Poem-of-the-Year" Contest 2013

"Five Day Visit" – Shortlisted for Arc's "Poem-of-the-Year" Contest 2012

—

"Let Us" was written for students at Chatelech Secondary School in Sechelt and presented with music, photos, and video.

"Sometimes" was produced with voice, music and images for inclusion in the 2021 Virtual Seedy Saturday Conference (Victoria, BC) and can be viewed on Youtube here: https://www.youtube.com/watch?v=U4E06bSBb-U I'm indebted to Rhona McAdam for her help with this.

Helen Humphrey's quote is from her novel *Wild Dogs* (Phyllis Bruce Books/HarperCollins, 2004).

Jan Zwicky's line appears in "Courage," from her poetry collection *The Long Walk* (University of Regina Press, 2016).

The Tony Hoagland (d. 2018) line is from his poem "Reasons to Survive November." It was published in *What Narcissism Means to Me* (Graywolf Press, 2003). An audio version of the poem, in Hoagland's voice, can he heard here:
https://poets.org/poem/reasons-survive-november-audio-only

The Ross Gay quote from his poem "To the Fig Tree on 9th and Christian" appears in his multi-award-winning book *Catalog of Unabashed Gratitude* (University of Pittsburgh Press, 2015).

———

Several of the *Go* poems found their way—with original music and/or the covers I attempted—into my 3-season podcast, Something Like Love. You can find the podcast here:
https://www.youtube.com/channel/UCsXEy0TyqqTwdzxXMUTc9Ag

Gratitude to the Alberta Foundation for the Arts for a grant in 2013-2014 while I was living in Edmonton. I am also indebted to the Writers' Trust of Canada for the George Woodcock Fund Grant in December 2021, when I needed to be in Saskatchewan with family.

I am grateful to live, write, and play on the traditional territory of the Coast Salish peoples, specifically Stz'uminus First Nation, whose historical relationships with the land continue to this day.

PHOTO CREDIT TO CAT MCPHAIL GAGNON

Shelley A. Leedahl is the author of thirteen books, including four previous poetry collections; an adult and a juvenile novel; short story collections; creative nonfiction; and the illustrated children's books *The Bone Talker* and *The Moon Watched It All*. She also writes for commercial markets, worked as a radio advertising copywriter in AB and SK, and writes dozens of book reviews annually. Leedahl has been awarded International Fellowships for prestigious artist residencies in the US, Mexico, Spain, and Scotland. She presents across the country. In 2020 she received a Canada Council for the Arts' Digital Originals Grant for her literary and musical podcast "Something Like Love". Shelley lives in Ladysmith, BC, and is often on hiking trails or in her kayak. writersunion.ca/member/shelleya-leedahl